"I love....."
Affirmations for a life worth living

Written and illustrated by Jen Tiller

Themes for "I love...."
Affirmations for a life worth living

Abundance

Calm

Assertiveness

Living Fully

Self-nurturing

Awareness

Intuition

Health

Choice

Balance

Learning

My world

Perspective

Rejuvenation

Being Centred

Relationships

Fun

Release

Happiness

Self-expression

Spirituality

Income

Confidence

Mindfulness

Energy

Breathing

Body Awareness

Serenity

Connections

Sleep

Self-esteem

Security

Clarity

Emotions

Grace

Law of Attraction

Introduction: using "I love...." Affirmations

What ARE affirmations? Any statement (positive OR negative) that reinforces a belief about an experience.   Positive affirmations are designed to improve habitual thoughts and encourage desired behaviours, until they are natural to us, springing from healthier unconscious beliefs. We aren't born with beliefs or expectations, we learn them. If the ones you have acquired don't serve you now, you CAN replace them with more helpful ones!

However, if there is a big difference between what you tell yourself and how you feel, there can be a sense of conflict and struggle.   If you feel sad, but affirm 'I AM happy' the statement lacks integrity.   There is often a response of 'that just isn't true' and it can feel quite uncomfortable - it can be difficult to use. Not the effect we want at all!

The "I love + an active verb" form of affirmations came into being with two shifts in my awareness. The first was so obvious - love is the ultimate creative force We already feel warmly towards whatever we think of with love (a pet, a favourite place or person etc) whether we are with them or not, and that emotion bridges the mental and emotional gap between where we are and where we're intending to go! We are truly drawn like a magnet to what we love.

We are more likely to take action to achieve goals we love.   When we hold these goals lovingly and naturally in our hearts, our world view shifts, our behaviours change, as we notice and attract the opportunities needed to create the life we CHOOSE.

When I played with starting all my affirmations with "I love....." it made a profound difference straight away. The second shift was when I found that using a verb (having, creating, receiving) in the affirmation makes it a living, active process, stated in the eternal now. Compare telling yourself 'I am healthy' with 'I love being healthy'. The first only feels completely true if you are healthy at the time. The second can be said at any point - it's always true. Any conflict around the affirmation vanishes, so mind and body can integrate and process the statement usefully, reinforcing health as a belief.

I've grouped these affirmations into topics. Each page is effectively a mini-workshop, giving you a deeper resonance with the theme as you move down the page, and repeating the core statement again at the end. The images (some of my favourite photos I've taken over the years) have been carefully chosen to relate to each set of affirmations - I hope they bring you as much pleasure as they have given me!

There is no right or wrong way to use these affirmations. Say them, write them, sing them, think them - whatever works for you! They are particularly useful in association with EFT (Emotional Freedom Technique, otherwise known as tapping.) Feel free to adjust them to suit your personal circumstances; enjoy creating your own from the suggestions on the Law of Attraction page and go from there.

May you have a life filled with love, light and laughter!

Jen Tiller

Abundance

I love creating a life full of abundance.
I love feeling everything I desire is available to me.
I love having abundant love, joy, health, wealth and energy.
I love freeing my mind from limitations.
I love being part of the every growing supply of
information, resources and energy.

I love choosing to receive with grace.
I love having the resources to give freely.
I love attracting opportunities for joy and success.
I love being aware of infinite possibilities.
I love nurturing the planet as I create a fulfilling life.
I love helping others to live abundantly fulfilling lives.

I love creating a life full of abundance.

Calm

I love being calm.
I love choosing to slow my thoughts.
I love allowing my muscles to soften and
ease into relaxation.
I love noticing my breathing become gentle and slow.
I love creating an oasis of calm in my mind and life.
I love feeling my eyes relax and my field of vision widen.

I love thinking clearly and easily as I experience calm.
I love softly accepting calm into my life.
I love noticing my movements become
slower and smoother.
I love finding the still, quiet place between the breaths.
I love sending out drifts of calm to relax
everyone around me.

I love knowing calm is something I can choose at any time.
I love being calm.

Assertiveness

I love being calmly assertive.

I love replacing confrontation or avoidance with calm discussion.

I love choosing healthy responses to both praise and criticism.

I love creating rapport and building trust by listening well.

I love using factual statements, open questions and calm body language as I express my thoughts and feelings.

I love knowing I am neither victim nor bully.

I love knowing I deserve to be heard.

I love showing respect to myself and others.

I love maintaining healthy boundaries to keep myself safe.

I love moving from past blame to present choice, creating a better future for all concerned.

I love being calmly assertive.

Living Fully

I love living a wonderful life.
I love discovering how often I can feel wonder and delight.
I love focusing on each moment, savouring every experience.
I love being curious, excited and full of wonder about the opportunities that surround me.

I love choosing to be grateful for everything that happens.
I love being stretched and challenged enough to learn and grow easily.
I love noticing beauty and love everywhere I go.
I love doing things that reflect my authentic self.

I love living a wonderful life.

Self-nurturing

I love choosing to nurture myself.
I love saying "Yes!" to what's good for me.
I love replacing self-criticism with positive, supportive words.
I love nourishing myself with healthy diet, exercise and habits.
I love giving myself the time and space to be me.

I love setting boundaries clearly, for myself and others.
I love recognising and transforming limiting ideas about my life.
I love learning to understand and accept myself as I grow.
I love giving myself the gift of unconditional love.
I love praising and rewarding myself for taking action.

I love choosing to nurture myself.

Awareness

I love paying attention to life with my whole being.
I love using my senses joyfully.
I love noticing the beauty in textures, shapes and patterns.
I love noticing light and colour and form.
I love exploring different ways to move and stand.

I love paying attention to the way I feel at every level.
I love choosing how closely I pay attention.
I love observing people and events with curiosity.
I love being truly present and aware.
I love experiencing pleasure.
I love noticing if I'm living in accordance with my values.

I love paying attention to life with my whole being.

Balance

I love creating a balanced life.
I love aligning my whole being - mind, body and spirit.
I love setting healthy priorities and acting on them.
I love balancing time and energy easily and efficiently.
I love moving easily and gracefully from my core.
I love being flexible and resourceful.

I love making decisions based on my values.
I love relaxing into peace and stillness.
I love having a balanced outlook on life.
I love enjoying food in healthy proportion to exercise and rest.
I love creating inner harmony.
I love experiencing my centre as a well-spring of love and peace.

I love creating a balanced life.

Intuition

I love developing my intuition.
I love paying attention to the clear voice of my inner wisdom.
I love noticing the differences between the pushy advice of
ego and the calm certainty of knowledge.
I love paying attention to the still, open place within.
I love learning to trust my intuition.

I love remembering I am truly connected at the
quantum level to everyone and everything.
I love discovering valuable patterns and connections in my life.
I love moving from coincidence to the spiritual connection of
synchronicity.
I love recognising signals from the universe that give genuine
guidance.

I love developing my intuition.

Choice

I love knowing I always have choices.
I love recognising the moment of choice between an event and my response.
I love realising that taking responsibility for my choices empowers me and helps me grow.
I love recognising when some choices are
AND rather than *OR.*

I love exploring the consequences of several choices before deciding.
I love choosing to act on my highest values.
I love being proactive.
I love being proud of my choices.
I love choosing to become my best self.

I love knowing I always have choices.

Health

I love being healthy.
I love feeling energetic and positive.
I love knowing my body has amazing powers to constantly
renew and regenerate.
I love radiating health and vitality through every cell and
system as I exercise and nourish myself.
I love being resilient and flexible.

I love creating a life of joy.
I love making healthy choices naturally and easily.
I love visualising every part of myself as glowing
with good health.
I love my body constantly creating a healthy immune system.
I love being grateful for every sign of my well-being.

I love being healthy.

Learning

I love learning easily.
I love having fun as I learn.
I love feeling wonder and curiosity.
I love exploring ways to learn with all of my senses.
I love recalling information easily.
I love learning as I share my knowledge.

I love gaining helpful knowledge from every experience.
I love finding great teachers and mentors.
I love seeing patterns and making connections.
I love having access to the knowledge I need.
I love making the most of my natural abilities.
I love exploring new ideas just for fun.

I love learning easily.

My world

I love creating a beautiful place to live.
I love being aware of space and light and energy.
I love enjoying gorgeous colours and scents and textures.
I love noticing the beauty in everyone and everything.
I love taking the time to enjoy art and architecture,
cloud shapes and flowers, clear air and shimmering water.

I love creating a welcoming space with kindness and smiles.
I love feeling good when I make eco-friendly choices.
I love feeling more at ease as I clear clutter from my space.
I love being aware of the beauty of nature in all its detail.
I love honouring this amazing planet.

I love creating a beautiful place to live.

Perspective

I love seeing the world from different viewpoints.
I love wondering… what *else* could this mean?
I love getting a laugh from looking at life from a new angle.
I love imagining events through the eyes of someonefrom the distant future or past.
I love reversing ideas and playing with possibilities.

I love wondering what opportunities and resources my favourite role model would notice.
I love recognising the difference between urgent and important.
I love remembering I can choose how I respond to life.

I love seeing the world from different viewpoints.

Rejuvenation

I love feeling rejuvenated.
I love knowing my whole body recreates itself constantly.
I love maintaining youthful energy throughout my life.
I love having strength and flexibility.
I love taking a fresh look at my life to create a wonderful present and future.

I love radiating the joy of life through every part of me.
I love giving my system all the nourishment it needs.
I love feeling refreshed and energised.
I love having a youthful outlook.
I love doing the day to day things that keep me youthful.

I love feeling rejuvenated.

Being Centred

I love being a centre of peace, integrity and happiness.
I love creating physical and emotional balance.
I love discovering the strength of my own emotional centre.
I love making all my decisions from my core values.
I love feeling an inner stillness from which to choose well.

I love noticing what improves my ability to remain centred.
I love radiating my intentions into the world.
I love shifting my attention to my heart and spirit.
I love recognising the value I offer the world right now.
I love connecting to other people at their true centre.

I love being a centre of peace, integrity and happiness.

Relationships

I love having healthy relationships.
I love choosing to surround myself with
supportive, honest, positive people.
I love learning how to recognise and nurture healthy
relationships of all kinds.
I love giving and receiving and sharing in balance.

I love setting healthy boundaries.
I love knowing I deserve wonderful relationships.
I love communicating with clarity and honesty.
I love choosing my response.
I love taking responsibility for my part of every relationship.

I love creating healthy relationships.

Fun

I love having fun.
I love feeling happy and playful.
I love dancing and singing freely and joyfully.
I love seeing the funny side of life.
I love having a light heart.

I love doing things just for fun.
I love seeing life through a child's eyes.
I love embracing opportunities to enjoy myself.
I love being grateful for the absurdities of life.
I love planning fun stuff into my life.

I love having fun.

Release

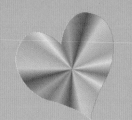

I love releasing outdated patterns easily.
I love feeling lighter as negative beliefs and habits are left behind.
I love ending the struggle to change the past.
I love freeing up my energy to create a better future.
I love replacing unforgiveness with unconditional love; 'shoulds' with acceptance; resentment with kindness.

I love recognising that every experience contains a valuable lesson
I love releasing unhelpful habits from my life.
I love moving into integrity and alignment with my higher purpose so positive change is inevitable.
I love allowing myself to be more flexible.

I love releasing outdate patterns easily.

Happiness

I love being happy.
I love seeing the world as a bright and cheerful place.
I love choosing to be happy for no particular reason.
I love creating a mindset where happiness is inevitable.
I love knowing I deserve to be happy and contented.
I love being with cheerful, positive people.

I love knowing what makes me happy and creating it often.
I love helping other people enjoy their lives too.
I love feeling warm and uplifted as I give freely
and receive joyfully.
I love taking responsibility for my own happiness.

I love being happy.

Self-expression

I love expressing myself clearly.
I love showing only my authentic self.
I love showing integrity in every word, choice and action.
I love telling others what I feel with honesty, respect
and sensitivity.
I love feeling comfortable with being open.

I love expressing myself in my clothes and personal style.
I love making my whole life an expression of my soul.
I love using language that helps others understand me.
I love being aware of my body language and tone of voice.
I love creating an inspired life.

I love expressing myself clearly.

Spirituality

I love connecting with my spiritual side.
I love being aware of my whole self and its larger existence.
I love recognising the part of me that is more than my physical experience.
I love discovering which spiritual path suit me best.
I love including spiritual practices naturally in my day.

I love discovering my spirit's purpose for being in this physical world.
I love feeling connected to and supported by the Source of all.
I love being at one with myself, balanced and aligned.
I love growing to understand my spiritual journey.
I love nurturing my spiritual side.

I love connecting with my spiritual side.

Income

I love having abundant income.
I love creating ongoing income from many
inspiring and ethical sources.
I love choosing to dip freely into the flow of
wealth in the world.
I love having all the resources I need available to me.
I love sharing my good fortune freely.

I love working with supportive, honest, enthusiastic,
knowledgeable people.
I love knowing I can always create more abundance.
I love enjoying whatever I do to create my income.
I love recognising opportunities and how to build on them.

I love having abundant income.

Confidence

I love feeling confident.
I love feeling centred and clear minded.
I love smiling as I create a positive image of future events.
I love speaking with enthusiasm.
I love choosing to enhance my skills.

I love discovering that confidence is a feeling I can choose.
I love knowing I can learn and improve every day.
I love being upright, with level chin and relaxed shoulders.
I love getting the best possible results from every situation.
I love having every reason to be optimistic.

I love feeling confident.

Mindfulness

I love living mindfully.
I love being aware of the way I think.
I love noticing the pattern of my thoughts.
I love choosing what I pay attention to.
I love making positive and beautiful images in my mind.

I love recognising the effects of my thoughts
on my experience.
I love paying attention and experiencing
each moment fully.
I love using my mind actively to create a better life.
I love thinking clearly and effectively.
I love using my whole mind deliberately.

I love living mindfully.

Energy

I love feeling energised.
I love feeling energy flowing through my whole being.
I love exploring the uses of energy on many levels.
I love being energetic and passionate as I manifest my
goals and intentions.
I love maintaining a positive spiral of energy.
I love being resilient and positive.

I love feeling inspired and uplifted.
I love using my energy to heal and empower.
I love knowing that my energy follows my thoughts.
I love creating positive synergy.
I love connecting to my spiritual power source.

I love feeling energised.

Breathing

I love breathing well.
I love feeling my airways being comfortably open as air easily
flows through them.
I love using my breath to speak, laugh and sing joyfully.
I love relaxing as I breathe more slowly and silently.
I love breathing the right amount of air for my body's needs.

I love feeling the strength that comes from using my stomach
muscles to breathe.
I love breathing easily however active I am.
I love creating energy and stamina with slow, even breathing.
I love noticing the calm that comes from pausing for a moment
after I breathe out.
I love breathing with awareness.

I love breathing well.

Body talk

I love creating a great relationship with my body.
I love choosing to value and enjoy my body.
I love expanding the way I use all my senses so I enjoy
my life more.
I love giving my body the exercise, nourishment and rest it needs.
I love paying attention to what I eat and listening to my body.

I love replacing tension with ease and grace.
I love being playful.
I love noticing how I fit into the physical world.
I love paying attention to the feedback from my body.
I love learning how I can work in harmony with my body.
I love exploring ways to be more flexible and balanced.

*I love creating a great relationship
with my body.*

Serenity

I love radiating serenity.

I love feeling the peace of knowing I'm where I need to be
for now.

I love choosing to be content with this moment on my journey.

I love remaining in the moment as I create a beautiful future.

I love creating an oasis of calm in the centre of my being.

I love being part of the flow of life.

I love observing the way serenity enriches my life at
every level.

I love softly accepting serenity as part of my life.

I love noticing my thoughts find balance and ease.

I love connecting with the serenity of nature.

I love influencing others as I choose serenity and joy.

I love radiating serenity.

I love being able to sleep well.
I love slowing my thoughts as I prepare for sleep.
I love breathing slowly and calmly by gently using my stomach muscles.
I love creating beautiful images as I drift into pleasant dreams.
I love waking refreshed and alert.

I love releasing tension from my muscles, letting them become warm and soft.
I love creating a soothing bedtime ritual.
I love allowing myself to rest, whether or not I sleep.
I love allowing myself to sleep easily and deeply.
I love trusting myself to sleep peacefully wherever I am.

I love being able to sleep well.

Connections

I love creating positive connections.
I love connecting with wonderful people, places and opportunities.
I love developing all my relationships with honour and care.
I love being part of something much greater than myself.
I love being connected to my own heart and intuition.

I love releasing connections that no longer support my journey.
I love creating links of the heart, mind and soul.
I love welcoming healthy, mutually supportive relationships into my life.
I love giving and receiving smiles, compliments and respect.
I love opening myself to friendship.

I love creating positive connections.

Self-esteem

I love feeling special.
I love recognising my uniqueness.
I love valuing my special qualities.
I love understanding that I have a contribution to make.
I love choosing to appreciate my value every day.
I love recognising I deserve to live up to my full potential.

I love knowing that being me is a unique, extraordinary and
miraculous experience.
I love taking responsibility for my experiences in life.
I love giving myself permission to be everything I can be.
I love honouring myself and respecting my choices.
I love enjoying being me.

I love feeling special.

Security

I love feeling secure.
I love being strong, flexible and confident.
I love realising security is about how I view my place
in the world.
I love feeling secure enough to take useful risks.
I love being part of a network of supportive, caring people.

I love knowing I can be more, or less, open as I choose.
I love feeling able to live my life fully.
I love stretching my boundaries and developing new
strengths and skills.
I love discovering useful new ways to redefine security.
I love feeling secure in my identity as I change and grow.
I love creating a healthy buffer zone at every level.

I love feeling secure.

Clarity

I love having a clear mind.
I love having a clear vision of my goals and outcomes.
I love focusing on each moment, savouring every experience.
I love allowing myself to explore reality without judgement.
I love being curious, excited and full of wonder about everything.
I love asking questions and being truly open to the answers.

I love gaining perspective by using someone else's point of view.
I love seeing my future as a matter of choice.
I love seeing the light in everything.
I love expressing my self clearly.
I love doing things that reflect my authentic self.
I love paying attention with all my senses.

I love having a clear mind.

Emotions

I love creating a healthy emotional life.
I love remembering that emotions are simply **E**nergy in *motion*.
I love being clear about my emotions and their real causes.
I love understanding the way my thoughts affect my feelings.
I love knowing I can move through strong emotion safely.
I love choosing my response to a trigger event.
I love learning to open my heart and remain whole.

I love doing things that naturally improve my mood.
I love finding safe and useful ways to channel energy.
I love understanding that my emotions are a useful compass for aligning me to my spiritual direction and life purpose.
I love allowing myself to find healthy ways to express my feelings.
I love releasing emotional baggage and responding to the present.

I love creating a healthy emotional life.

Grace

I love living gracefully.
I love being aware of every movement flowing easily.
I love moving calmly and smoothly.
I love feeling the lightness that comes as I lift myself to my full
height and smile.
I love freeing myself from tension and limitation
to make room for something better.
I love discovering a sense of grace and gratitude in every day life.

I love having the grace to release past hurts and move on.
I love allowing loving energy to freely flow from my heart outwards.
I love moving in harmony with my heart and soul.
I love dealing with others with courtesy and kindness.
I love sharing my gifts with the world.

I love living gracefully.

Law of attraction

I love knowing that whatever I pay attention to, grows.
I love finding many ways to complete these affirmations:

I love attracting...
I love creating...
I love understanding...
I love giving...
I love easily learning...
I love feeling...
I love connecting with...
I love becoming more
   relaxed about...
I love living in...
I love exploring new
   ways to...
I love discovering...
I love receiving...

I love releasing...
I love replacing... with...
I love saying loving things
   to myself about...
I love owning...
I love being a great
   role model for...
I love improving...
I love being surrounded by...
I love choosing...
I love enjoying...
I love realising I am...
I love empowering myself by...
I love improving...

I love knowing that whatever I pay attention to, grows.

If you feel it's time to change your thinking, release old patterns, improve your health or perhaps gain new skills and support in your professional life, please get in touch with Jen.

About the author: Jen Tiller

After recovering from decades of severe health problems, including asthma and agoraphobia, Jen trained in many of the techniques that had changed her own life. Becoming a therapist, trainer, author and speaker, she now devotes her life to increasing awareness, health and resilience with practical, inspiring and life changing programmes.

Jen offers 1-1 therapy, workshops, mentoring and resources such as a inspirational journals, affirmations posters and books, relaxation CDs, as well as art and photography for creating peaceful spaces.

The Resilient Therapist Programme is Jen's way of supporting people who give of themselves day after day (medical staff, carers, complementary therapists, social workers, teachers...it's a long list!) to feel great as they make a difference. After all, you can't give what you don't have!

Jen is an EFT practitioner, NLP Trainer,
Buteyko breathing therapist,   Reiki Master Teacher,
author, artist, speaker, and winner of the
BEW Innovation award.

Contact Jen for details of workshops, 1-1 sessions, mentoring and resources:

jentiller@realityquest.co.uk

www.jentiller.co.uk

Twitter   @jentiller
            @healerzone
Facebook   Jen Tiller

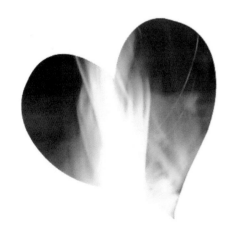

Picture: Jen with Nina, a snow leopard cub at the Cat Survival Trust, Hertfordshire, UK where she volunteers. Ask about her 'talk and tour' events.
Image: Mark Tiller   www.catsurvivaltrust.org